USS Wisconsin BB-64

Hampton Roads Naval Museum
Photo Museum Guide
By Randall S. Shoker

Hampton Roads Naval Historical Foundation

Dom Menta

Wisconsin in full flag dress in the early 1950's

This book is dedicated to the brave men and women in the United States armed forces and the sacrifices they make, and have made, to keep this the land of the free and the home of the brave.

Copyright 2003 by Randall S. Shoker
All rights reserved. No part of this book may be reproduced without written permission by the author.
Drawings by Chelsea E. Shoker and Randall S. Shoker
Text Editor William F. Fisher

ISBN #1-930127-05-7
2nd Printing June 2005
Published by the Oxford Museum Press, Inc. Oxford, Ohio
Printed in Cincinnati, Ohio by T.L. Krieg Offsett Inc.

Overleaf U.S. Navy

Wisconsin *steaming in the western Pacific during her eight-month deployment in World War II. She is wearing the measure 22 camouflage that she would wear the entire war.*

Contents

National Archives

Wisconsin *under construction on January 12, 1943, looking forward. She is about 35% complete at this point.*

Battleship Wisconsin BB-64

Design and History

In late 1937, as the global arms race was heating up, the U.S. Navy grew increasingly nervous about the ability of its new battleships to stand up to the warships under construction in Japan. Of particular concern was the Naval Intelligence report from Italian sources that Japan was building three super battleships.

If this were true, it would render the entire American battleship fleet, including the new battleships that were planned, obsolete. As a precaution, in late 1937 the Navy began to investigate what kind of ship could be built on a displacement of 45,000 tons. Diplomatically, the United States, France, and Great Britain asked the Imperial Japanese Government to assure them that it would not build over the 35,000-ton limit imposed by the Second London Naval Treaty of 1936. On February 12, 1938, Japan gave Washington a vague and elusive answer. The U.S. immediately took Japan's answer as a no and invoked an escalator clause in the treaty allowing for 45,000 ton ships and 16-inch guns.

While the Navy was studying its design options, an unusual thing happened. President Roosevelt intervened directly in the design process. He told Secretary of the Navy Swanson that he wanted the biggest battleships in the world, with an unheard of top speed of 35 knots. Captain Allan J. Chantry, who had a master's degree in naval architecture from MIT, was largely responsible for the design of these magnificent new ships. There were to be four of them (six were planned, two eventually cancelled), and they were named for the lead ship in the class, the USS *Iowa*. On January 25, 1941, the fourth *Iowa*, the USS *Wisconsin*, was laid down in the Philadelphia Navy Yard.

As Captain Chantry set out to build the ships Roosevelt wanted, his design

Dom Menta

Wisconsin *squeezes through the Panama Canal in the 1950s.*

team knew that it did not have a totally free hand. The limitations of several major U.S. harbors and docks meant that the mighty ships could draw no more than thirty-six feet of water when fully loaded. Another major constraint on the ships' design was the absolute requirement that they be able to fit through the Panama Canal, which was 110 feet wide. While these constraints made the engineering work more difficult, Captain Chantry's final design was a landmark of naval architecture.

The *Iowa* class battleships had an unparalleled balance of offensive and defensive capabilities. The Mark 7, 16-inch, 50 caliber gun designed for the *Iowa*s has been called the most destructive naval gun ever to put to sea. Its longer barrel allowed greater muzzle velocity for the

Photographer Dom Menta catches two of Wisconsin*'s big 16-inch shells in flight in this dramatic photograph taken in the early 1950s.*

7

U.S. Navy

Wisconsin's big guns blast North Korean rail targets during Operations Package *and* Derail *in March 1952.* Package *and* Derail *were designed to destroy the North Korean rail line running down the east coast of Korea. During this operation,* Wisconsin *scored a direct hit on a steam locomotive with a 16-inch shell.*

massive 2,700 pound-armor piercing shells, giving them a destructive reach of over 23 nautical miles! The one drawback to the powerful new guns was the inability of the *Iowa*s to be armored against guns at least as powerful as they carried. It was not a critical design shortcoming; the Navy reasoned that if it could not armor a ship against the Mark 7 gun, no one else could either. The long graceful lines of the ships' hulls, combined with their massive power plants, allowed them to slice through the water in excess of 33 knots. Their large size allowed them to carry over 2.5 million gallons of fuel oil. That was enough to steam over 15,000 miles at a speed of 15 knots. With the modern Navy fuels of the 1980's and an overhaul of her boilers, Wisconsin's range was extended to 20,000 miles during her latest refit.

To say that the *Iowa*s were complex ships to build is an understatement. *Wisconsin* required almost 20,000 sets of working plans to complete her construction. It took 14,000 valves to operate her 42 miles of piping. Items as simple as lights were difficult. Five thousand light fixtures that could withstand the rigors of combat were needed as well as over 1,100 telephones. On top of that was the massive amount of labor to build the ship. It took 2,891,334 man days (the amount of work one man does in one day) to build *Wisconsin.*

In addition to the complexity of building the ships in peacetime, early wartime experience dictated changes to

Dom Menta

Wisconsin *(BB-64) is tied up next to her sister ship* New Jersey *(BB-62) in this unusual photo taken in 1954. Notice that* Wisconsin *has men over the side working and that both ships have their boat booms extended. The long, graceful lines of the ships are evident in this photo.*

the ships before they were done. Seemingly minor details, like the number of small anti-aircraft guns, caused major problems for Chantry. Just a few months after *Wisconsin* was laid down, the Navy Board decided to adopt the Swedish 40mm Bofors and the Swiss 20mm Oerlikon as its primary light anti-aircraft weapons. That required changes to the ship's electrical plans. But that was just the beginning. As the four ships were being built, the number of planned anti-aircraft guns grew, from the original "new" mandate of fifteen 40mm quad mounts to *Wisconsin's* eventual twenty 40mm quads. Other construction changes included electronics and radar. When WWII started, radar was in the primitive stages of development, but by the time the *Wisconsin* was commissioned, she was covered with new state-of-the-art electronic devices. An entirely new room, not in the original design, a CIC or combat information center, was added late in the construction process.

When finished, *Wisconsin* and her three sisters of the *Iowa* class were the finest capital ships ever built. The design proved flexible and the ships fulfilled missions that did not exist when they were designed. They were the only WWII capital ships capable of keeping up with the fast aircraft carriers in heavy seas, and their massive anti-aircraft gun batteries proved decisive in helping to protect those carriers. Their giant fuel tank capacity also allowed *Wisconsin* to act as a floating gas station to refuel other ships of the fleet. During the last eight months of WWII, *Wisconsin* refueled destroyers over 250 times.

With her large fuel capacity Wisconsin *became a floating fuel station at sea for the smaller ships. Here* Wisky *refuels the* George E. Davis, *a* John C. Butler *class destroyer escort during her 1950s deployment. The U.S. Navy's ability to refuel other ships while underway was a skill lost on most other navies of the world.*

National Archives

Wisconsin's after deck during a snowstorm on February 8, 1952, while serving with Task Force 77 in Korea. Her Sikorsky HO3S helicopter is secured on her fantail. A few days before, on February 4, Wisky's helicopter, flown by L.L. Barton, had attempted to rescue a downed Naval pilot in North Korean territory. The helicopter was hit by North Korean anti-aircraft fire and forced to retreat. Shot up and running low on fuel, Barton radioed Wisconsin with his position. Wisconsin cranked up to 27 knots and sailed toward the wounded aircraft in the darkness of night. Using a searchlight as a landing beacon, Wisconsin reached her stricken helicopter just in time--when the aircraft landed it had only three gallons of fuel left.

Perhaps the most important duty the ships performed, and the one that keeps *Wisconsin* on standby status to this day, was shore bombardment. *Wisconsin* cut her teeth during the invasion of Okinawa, where she, *New Jersey* and *Missouri* hit Japanese shore positions with their 16-inch guns. Later in the war, they would hit industrial targets on the Japanese mainland. The ships performed similar duties in Korea, Vietnam and the Persian Gulf.

Rebuilds and Refits

After her short career in WWII ended, *Wisky (Wisconsin's* nickname used by her crew) fulfilled various fleet duties until she was deactivated on July 1, 1948 at the Norfolk Naval Ship-yard. She was recommissioned on March 3, 1951 for duties in the Korean War, where she served with distinction. She was placed out of commission and in reserve again in March 1958. Her sister ship, the battleship *New Jersey,* was reactivated for the Vietnam War in 1969. All four of the great ships stayed in "mothballs" during the 1970's, and they survived several attempts for disposal. The U.S. Marine Corps was the ship's strongest advocate, arguing the need for the massive 16-inch guns in possible future wars. In 1981, the Reagan administration, faced with the growing might of the Soviet Navy, decided to reactivate all four ships.

On October 22, 1988, *Wisconsin* rejoined the U.S. Navy. While she had undergone a minor refit for the Korean War, she underwent a major modernization for her 1988 recommissioning. Her entire center superstructure was rebuilt to accommodate two powerful new weapons systems. She now carried thirty-two Tomahawk cruise missiles in eight armored box launchers, and she carried sixteen Harpoon anti-ship missiles. Anti-aircraft and close-in missile defense was now provided for by four Vulcan Phalanx guns. In addition she still carried six of her original ten 5in/38cal gun mounts, and of course all nine of the big 16-inch rifles.

With the collapse of the Soviet Union in 1990, it looked like *Wisconsin* would return to decommissioned status for a third time. But on August 2, 1990, Iraq invaded Kuwait, and five days later, *Wisconsin* left for the Persian Gulf. She made the 8,500 mile trip in just sixteen days. Five months later, she fired twenty-six Tomahawk cruise missiles in the first two days of the Gulf War. After her missile mission was done, she hit specific land-based targets, using her remotely piloted vehicle as a spotter aircraft. Once the ground war started, she provided fire support in a "call for fire" capacity for troops on the ground. She left the Gulf for home in March 1991, after providing excellent service to her country and the men and women on shore. On September 30, 1991, *Wisconsin* was decommissioned for a third time. She is now the charge of the Hampton Roads Naval Museum and is a memorial to honor for all time the men and women who served our country both in war and peace.

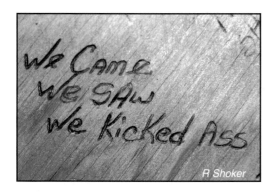

R Shoker

Above: When Wisconsin *was deactivated after her Gulf War deployment, the crew left many messages on the wooden covers used to protect machinery. Crew pride is evident in this message left on a cover in the forward plotting room.*

Unknown, provided by Barry Cordwell

Wisconsin *fires a Tomahawk cruise missile as her crew looks on during her last deployment.*

A Japanese bomber burns in this April 9, 1945 photo. Wisconsin's anti-aircraft guns throw up a wall of fire to protect the fleet.

U.S. Navy

USS Wisconsin BB-64
Service Highlights

July 6, 1939 Congress authorizes construction of third and fourth *Iowa* class battleships, USS *Missouri* and USS *Wisconsin*.

January 25, 1941 *Wisconsin*'s keel is laid down at Philadelphia Navy Yard.

December 7, 1943 *Wisconsin* is launched. She is sponsored by Mrs. Walter S. Goodland.

April 16, 1944 *Wisconsin* is commissioned.

July 7, 1944 *Wisky* leaves Norfolk for a shakedown cruise to Trinidad followed by a re-work period in the Philadelphia Navy Yard for repairs and adjustments.

October 2, 1944 *Wisconsin* joins the Pacific Fleet.

December 9, 1944 *Wisconsin* arrives in Ulithi and is assigned to the Third Fleet, commanded by Admiral William F. Halsey.

US Navy

Wisconsin*'s crane lifts one of the ship's Kingfisher aircraft from the water during the closing days of WWII. A wartime censor has removed all of* Wisconsin*'s radars and sensors from the photo, and her name as well.*

January 3, 1945   Protects carriers during air strikes against Formosa, Luzon and a mission into the South China Sea.

February 16, 1945   Joins Admiral Spruance's Task Force 58 to protect carriers as U.S. Navy aircraft struck the Japanese coast.

February 19, 1945   Provides fire support for landings on Iwo Jima: *Wisconsin's* first combat of the war.

March 19, 1945   Provides protection for the heavily damaged aircraft carrier *Franklin. Franklin* is almost sunk by one of the most savage kamikaze attacks of the war.

March 24, 1945   *Wisconsin* joins her sisters *New Jersey* and *Missouri* in the bombardment of Okinawa.

May 28, 1945   Escorts carriers during air attacks on Japanese mainland.

July 15, 1945   Shells steel mills and oil refineries at Muroran, Hokkaido.

July 17, 1945   Destroys the industrial site in Hitachi Miro with 16-inch gunfire.

August 13, 1945   Provides protection for aircraft carriers in final air strike on Tokyo.

September 5, 1945   Arrives in Tokyo Bay as part of occupying fleet.

September 23, 1945   Leaves Okinawa for the United States, joining in Operation Magic Carpet to bring soldiers home from the war.

Spring 1947   Takes a two-week cruise to train Naval reservists.

June - July 1947   Sails to northern European waters to train new midshipmen.

July 1, 1948   Is placed out of commission, in reserve, and is assigned to Norfolk Group of Atlantic Reserve Fleet.

March 3, 1951   Is recommissioned.

U.S. Navy Photo courtesy of George Kent

An unexpected mission that the Wisconsin*'s floatplanes filled was rescuing downed pilots. Eventually helicopters would excel in this role, but the floatplanes pioneered air rescue. Here, pilot George Travis prepares to hook up his Kingfisher for retrieval by* Wisconsin*'s crane after rescuing LTJG R. L. Meltebeke.*

November 26, 1951 Departs Yokosuka, Japan for Korea to support air operations of Task Force 77.

December 2, 1951 Provides ground gunfire support for South Korean troops in Kasong-Donsong.

December 3-6, 1951 Supports 1st Marine Division with gunfire. Destroys T-34 tank with a direct hit, as well as gun emplacements, artillery positions, enemy bunkers and troops.

December 11, 1951 Returns to Kasong-Kosong area and destroys enemy ground positions.

December 14, 1951 Provides UN troops with gunfire support in Kojo area.

December 16, 1951 Sails for Sasebo, Japan to re-arm.

December 18, 1951 Provides gunfire support for 11th ROK Division with night fire helping the South Koreans to push back a North Korean attack.

December 20-22, 1951 Shells targets at harbor in Wonson.

January 11, 1952 Provides gunfire support for 1st Marine Division and 1st ROK (South Korean Army) Corps.

January 26, 1952 Shells targets in Kojo area in conjunction with an air attack, then hits North Korean artillery sites in Hodo Pando.

March 15, 1952 Attacks North Korean railway at Songjin, destroying troop train. *Wisconsin* receives her first direct hit when a starboard 40mm mount is struck by a shell from a 152mm gun battery. In the famous "Temper, Temper" incident, *Wisconsin* turns her 16-inch guns on the enemy battery and completely destroys it.

March 19, 1952 Arrives back in Japan.

April 1, 1952 *Wisky* is relieved as flagship of the Seventh Fleet by her sister, *Iowa* and sails for the United States.

June, 1952 Takes midshipmen on a training cruise to Scotland, France and Cuba.

August 25, 1952 Sails to participate in NATO exercise, Operation *Mainbrace* in the North Atlantic.

Summer 1953 Another midshipmen training cruise, this time south to Brazil, Trinidad and Cuba.

October 12, 1953 Back to the east, *Wisconsin* relieves her sister *New Jersey* as flagship of Seventh Fleet.

Winter 1953 Visits ports of Yokosuka, Kobe, Nagasaki, Otaru and Sasebo in Japan.

April 1, 1954 Is relieved of flagship duties and returns to United States.

July 12, 1954 Sails to Scotland, France and Cuba on a midshipmen training cruise.

Summer 1955 Another midshipmen training cruise. *Wisconsin* called on ports in Scotland, Denmark and Cuba.

"Temper, Temper!"

On March 15, 1952, while shelling the enemy railway at Songjin, *Wisconsin* was hit (right) by what was thought to be a 152mm shell from an ex-Soviet artillery piece (below). Suffering three men wounded, *Wisky* immediately turned her 16-inch guns on the offending battery and destroyed it. Her quick shooting prompted the signal "Temper, Temper!" from an escorting destroyer.

Vyacheslav Ryzhenkov

Perry Bodnar

May 6, 1956   In heavy fog *Wisconsin* collides with the destroyer *Eaton*.

May 13, 1956   Is dry-docked at Norfolk Navy Yard to repair massive damage to her bow. *Wisconsin*'s bow is replaced with 68ft long section of bow of uncompleted sister battleship *Kentucky* that had been carried by barge from Newport News.

July 9, 1956   With her new bow in place, takes NROTC on a training cruise to Spain, Scotland and Cuba.

March 27, 1957   Leaves for the Mediterranean.

June 19, 1957   Leaves for her last midshipmen training cruise in the 1950s. She sails through the Panama Canal and in South American waters.

March 8, 1958   *Wisconsin* is decommissioned at Bayonne. The U.S. Navy is without an active battleship for the first time since 1895. When the Bayonne facility is closed, *Wisconsin* is towed to Philadelphia.

August 8, 1986   Leaves Philadelphia to go to the Avondale Shipyard in New Orleans for modernization and reactivation.

October 22, 1988   *Wisconsin* is recommissioned for the third time. Is rearmed with tomahawk and harpoon missiles. She and her sisters are the most formidable ships ever to put to sea.

August 7, 1990   *Wisky* is ordered to proceed to the Persian Gulf to help contain Saddam Hussein after his invasion of Kuwait. *Wisconsin* makes the trip in 16 days.

January 17, 1991   In position on the firing line as *Tomahawk Strike Warfare Commander* for the Persian Gulf, she launches 24 Tomahawk cruise missiles in a 48 hour period at Iraqi targets.

February 6, 1991   *Wisconsin* begins strategic shore bombardment of Iraqi targets.

February 24, 1991   *Wisconsin* provides gunfire support for ground troops in their drive to push Saddam's troops from Kuwait.

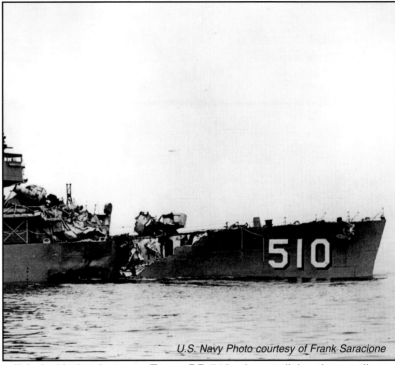

U.S. Navy Photo courtesy of Frank Saracione

U.S. Navy Photo courtesy of Frank Saracione

Cruising in heavy fog on May 6, 1956, Wisconsin *collided with the destroyer* Eaton *DD 510, almost slicing the smaller ship's bow off and cutting a gash six feet below her waterline. The* Eaton *suffered one casualty and flooding in her forward engine room.* Wisconsin *suffered no casualties but sustained major damage to her bow. Both ships returned to Norfolk for emergency repairs.*

U.S. Navy Photo courtesy of Frank Saracione

R. Shoker

Norfolk Naval Shipyard replaced the damaged 68 foot bow section from her unfinished sister, the battleship Kentucky. Wisconsin *was back at sea in an amazing 16 days.*

February 24, 1991 *Wisconsin* provides gunfire support for ground troops in their drive to push Saddam's troops from Kuwait.

September 30, 1991 *Wisconsin* is decommissioned for the third time.

April 16, 2001 *Wisconsin* opens for visitors in Norfolk.

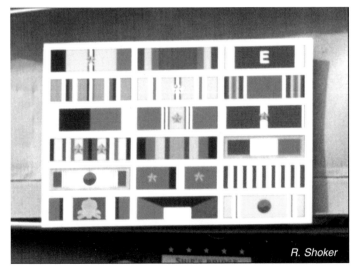

Wisconsin's Ribbon Board

USS Wisconsin Battle Awards

1st Row - Combat Action Ribbon with one gold star (WWII and Korea), Navy Unit Commendation, Battle "E"

2nd Row - American Campaign Medal, Asiatic Pacific Campaign with silver star in lieu of five battle stars, WWII Victory Medal

3rd Row - Navy Occupation Medal, National Defense Service Medal with one bronze star, Korean Service Medal with one battle star

4th Row - Southwest Asia Service Medal with two battle stars (Desert Shield and Desert Storm), Sea Service Deployment Ribbon, Philippine Presidential Unit Citation

5th Row - Korean Presidential Unit Citation, Philippine Ribbon with two battle stars, United Nations Service Medal

6th Row – Liberation Medal – Saudi Arabia, Kuwait Liberation Medal- Kuwait, Republic of Korea Medal

Armament

Dom Menta

Mark 7   16-inch/50 Caliber Rifle

The 3-gun turret for Wisconsin*'s Mark 7, 16-inch guns. The turret could fire six shells per minute and was accurate to ranges of over twenty miles.* Wisconsin*'s guns were deadly against shore targets in three wars. These drawings represent* Wisconsin*'s turret 1 during the Korean War. Right : Plan view of number 1 turret. Below: Profile view showing a cross section of the gun's mounting on* Wisconsin

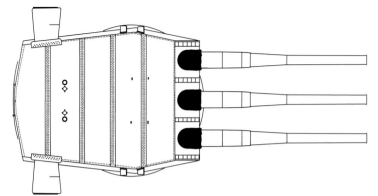

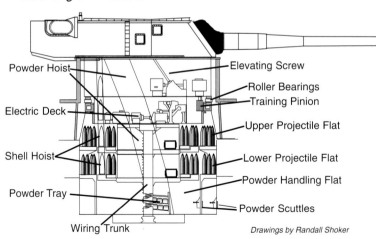

Powder Hoist
Electric Deck
Shell Hoist
Powder Tray
Wiring Trunk

Elevating Screw
Roller Bearings
Training Pinion
Upper Projectile Flat
Lower Projectile Flat
Powder Handling Flat
Powder Scuttles

Drawings by Randall Shoker

The main armament of *Wisconsin* and her sisters is the Mark 7, a 16-inch/50 caliber Naval gun. Designed especially for the *Iowa*s, it is considered the most versatile and destructive naval gun ever to put to sea. It was a significant improvement over the 16-inch/45 caliber guns of the prior *North Carolina* and *South Dakota* classes.

Wisconsin carries nine of these massive rifles in three armored turrets, two forward and one aft, containing three guns each.

The guns can elevate and fire individually. Each turret weighs around 2,200 tons, as much as a World War II destroyer! The barrels are chromium plated and are rifled with 96 grooves, twisting once in 25 calibers or 33.3 feet.

The Mark 7 gun fires two basic rounds, armor piercing and high explosive. For use against other battleships and hardened targets, the Mark 7 can fire a 2,700 pound AP (armor piercing) shell. With a full charge, this shell had a muzzle velocity of 2,425 feet per second, and a maximum range of 40,185 yards, or about 23 statute miles. For use against "soft" targets, *Wisconsin* fired a 1,900 pound HC (high capacity) shell. This shell was her primary weapon against land targets and came in many different configurations (a total of twelve) depending on the target. During World War II and Korea, *Wisconsin* usually fired the shells at reduced powder loads to save barrel wear. Each barrel would wear out after firing about 290 rounds. In the 1980s and 1990s, the Navy switched to special wear-reducing jackets for the powder bag, extending barrel life to an estimated 1,500 rounds.

To fire each shell at full charge, it took six 110-pound silk bags of propellant loaded behind each shell. The bags were made of silk so they would burn away after each shot. To ensure that there was no burning residue, each gun got cleared with a 175 psi blast of air after each firing.

All turrets were designed to work with the ship's highly advanced fire control systems, but they also had their own fire control equipment and could be locally controlled in an emergency. A well-trained crew could fire two rounds per minute per barrel, no small feat considering that a 2,700 pound shell had to be brought up from the magazines below, loaded in the gun, then six 110 pound bags of powder put in place. The gun was then elevated to precise coordinates. The performance of the big guns itself was a tribute to the professionalism and competence of the sailors and officers of *Wisconsin*.

BGM 109 Tomahawk Cruise Missile

R. Shoker

BGM 109 Tomahawk cruise missile

Drawing by Chelsea Shoker

The biggest increase in *Wisconsin's* offensive firepower came during her 1988 reactivation, when she received the Tomahawk weapons system. *Wisconsin* carried thirty-two of the powerful Tomahawk cruise missiles in eight armored box launchers of four missiles each. Armed with her new missiles, *Wisconsin* now carried a precision guided weapon that could deliver a conventional warhead to targets up to 675 miles away. Tomahawks could also carry a nuclear warhead to a target up to 1,500 miles away. The missiles had a cruising speed of .5 mach (mach is the speed of sound) and an attack speed of .75 mach.

Left: *The business end of the Tomahawk ABL launchers (armored box launchers). Each launcher holds four missiles in a separate canister. When firing, the center section elevates and the rear doors open to vent exhaust gas. See the launch photo on page 15.*

29

RGM 84 Harpoon Anti-Ship Missile

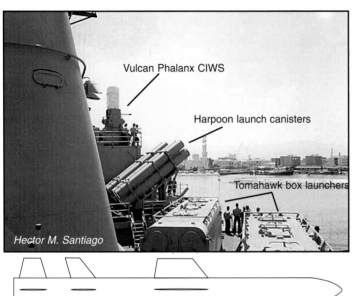

Vulcan Phalanx CIWS

Harpoon launch canisters

Tomahawk box launchers

Hector M. Santiago

RGM Harpoon anti-ship missile with fins extended for flight.

Drawing by Chelsea Shoker

In addition to the mighty Tomahawks, *Wisconsin* carried sixteen Harpoon anti-ship cruise missiles. This gave *Wisconsin* an over-the-horizon strike capability against enemy ships. They were carried in four Mark 141 launchers with four missiles each. Two of these launchers are visible in the center of the photo at left. Each tube held one Harpoon missile. Upon launch, the missile's fins extended from their folded position as the weapon left its tube. The Harpoon carried its warhead to a maximum range of 85 nautical miles at a maximum speed of .87 mach. The Harpoon is still considered to be one of the most effective anti-ship missiles in the U.S. Navy's arsenal.

5 inch/38 caliber Dual-purpose gun

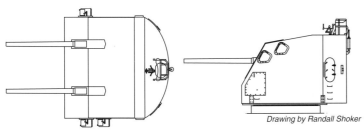

Drawing by Randall Shoker

R. Shoker

   This 5-inch/38 caliber gun was perhaps the best dual purpose gun (against both surface and aircraft targets) of World War II. The mount excelled in accuracy, barrel life, speed of movement, and perhaps most importantly, rate of fire. It was mounted in virtually every major warship built or rebuilt during the war. *Wisconsin* carried twenty of these guns in ten 2-gun mounts during her service in WWII and Korea. During her most recent activation, four 2-gun mounts were removed to make room for her new missile batteries.

Wisconsin *still retains six of her original ten 5inch/38 caliber mounts. They are currently in a state of preservation.*

31

R. Shoker

Vulcan Phalanx CIWS

As the Soviet Navy developed powerful new anti-ship missiles in the 1960s, the U.S. Navy sought to develop a last ditch missile defense system to counter Soviet threats. The result was the Vulcan Phalanx CIWS (Close-In Weapon System). The CIWS was a self contained unit that could be bolted anywhere on the ship. The unit had its own pulse doppler radar that tracked and engaged high-speed targets (under the white plastic dome) and fired up to 3,000 rounds per minute from its 6-barreled Gatling gun. *Wisconsin* carried four CIWS's that provided full 360-degree protection for the ship. They were removed when the ship was deactivated.

A CIWS system mounted on a Coast Guard Cutter.

40mm Bofors anti-aircraft guns -- WWII and Korea

Dom Menta

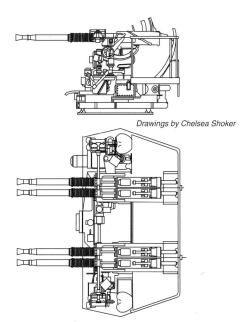

Drawings by Chelsea Shoker

This water-cooled gun was the main close-range anti-aircraft weapon for the U.S. Navy in World War II. *Wisconsin* carried twenty quadruple 40mm mounts from WWII through her deactivation in 1958. The ammunition was hand-loaded so the guns could never hope to live up to their sustained maximum rate of fire of 160 rounds per minute.

Ballistic Data 40mm Bofors
Bore: 1.575 inches
Length OA: 148.8 inches
Barrel life: approx. 9,500 rounds
Shell weight: 1.985 pounds
Max. range: 11,000 yards
Firing cycle: 160 rounds per minute

33

20mm Oerlikon anti-aircraft guns -- WWII

Marshall. Pearson

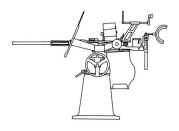

Drawings by Chelsea Shoker

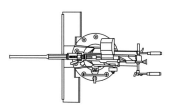

In November 1940, the U.S. Navy adopted the Swiss 20mm air-cooled gun as a last ditch defense against enemy aircraft. It enjoyed a good reputation until it proved totally inadequate against kamikazes. The gun was very lightweight, had a small footprint, and could be placed about anywhere on the ship. In 1945, *Wisconsin* carried forty-nine single mounts and eight twin mounts. They were all removed by 1947.

Ballistic Data   20mm Oerlikon

Bore:	.7874 inches
Length OA:	87 inches
Barrel life:	approx. 9,000 rounds
Shell weight:	.271 pounds
Muzzle Velocity:	2,740 feet per second
Max. range:	4,800 yards
Rate of fire:	450 rounds per minute

Radar and Fire Control

When *Wisconsin* was authorized, radar was in its infancy. By the time she was under construction, it became clear that not only was radar a useful new tool, it was absolutely necessary to protect the ship from attacking aircraft and also in helping hit enemy targets. As *Wisconsin* was a new ship, she received the very latest in radar when she was built and every time she was reactivated. As built, she had basically three different types of radar: SK (air search), SG (surface search), and ranging radars on top of the directors for the 5-inch guns and the main 16-inch batteries.

Radar played a vital role during WWII and Korea, and was still important during her Gulf War deployment. While some of the equipment has been removed, most of it is still on the ship. The schematic on page 37 shows some of *Wisconsin's* radars and sensors that were in use during her last deployment.

American naval fire control is the best in the world. On Wisconsin, the U.S. Navy used the director system to direct gunfire using optics, radar, and both analog and digital fire control computers. There were two plotting rooms that contained the fire control equipment for the main guns, and two for the secondary guns. Data was fed to these plotting rooms from two Mk 38 main battery directors for the 16in/50 cal. main guns and four Mk 37 directors for the 5in/38 cal.

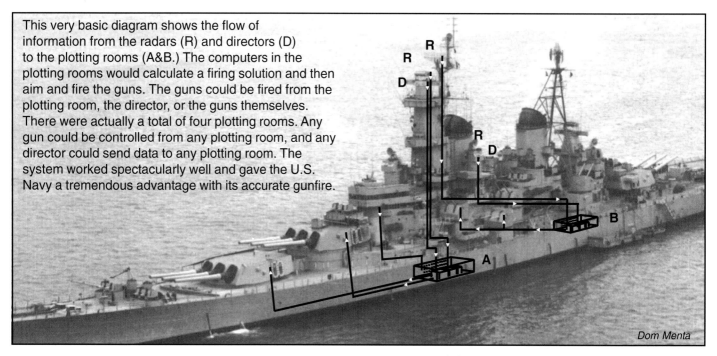

This very basic diagram shows the flow of information from the radars (R) and directors (D) to the plotting rooms (A&B.) The computers in the plotting rooms would calculate a firing solution and then aim and fire the guns. The guns could be fired from the plotting room, the director, or the guns themselves. There were actually a total of four plotting rooms. Any gun could be controlled from any plotting room, and any director could send data to any plotting room. The system worked spectacularly well and gave the U.S. Navy a tremendous advantage with its accurate gunfire.

Dom Menta

secondary guns. *Wisconsin* was designed to fight other battleships, so every possible backup was built into the system. Any one of the three main turrets or any secondary gun could be controlled from any director or plotting room in an emergency. As a last resort, the guns could go to local control, meaning each gun aimed and shot by itself.

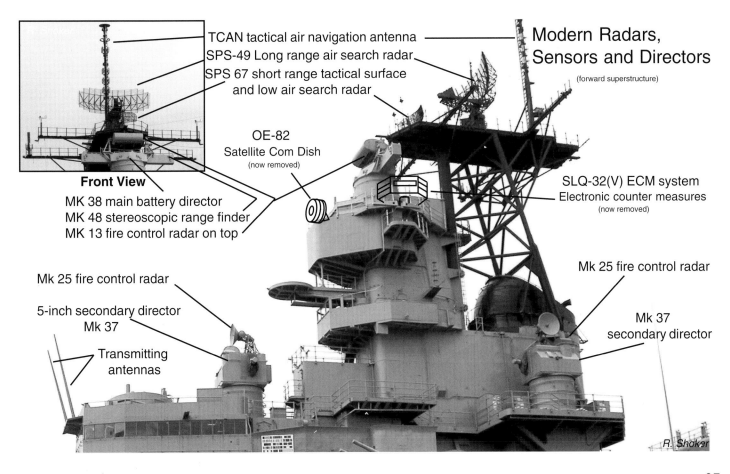

TCAN tactical air navigation antenna

SPS-49 Long range air search radar

SPS 67 short range tactical surface and low air search radar

Modern Radars, Sensors and Directors
(forward superstructure)

OE-82
Satellite Com Dish
(now removed)

SLQ-32(V) ECM system
Electronic counter measures
(now removed)

Front View

MK 38 main battery director
MK 48 stereoscopic range finder
MK 13 fire control radar on top

Mk 25 fire control radar

5-inch secondary director
Mk 37

Transmitting antennas

Mk 25 fire control radar

Mk 37
secondary director

R. Shoker

37

Mk 37 secondary director

Mk 37 secondary director

Harpoon missile racks

Armored Conning tower

Tomahawk missile launchers

5in/38cal gun mounts

R. Shoker

A portrait view of the port (left) side of Wisconsin*'s forward and mid superstructure with various features listed.*

A detailed view of the starboard (right) side of Wisconsin's aft superstructure showing the refueling equipment used to send fuel while underway. The helicopter control station not only directed flight operations for all helicopters, but also for the unmanned RPV scout aircraft.

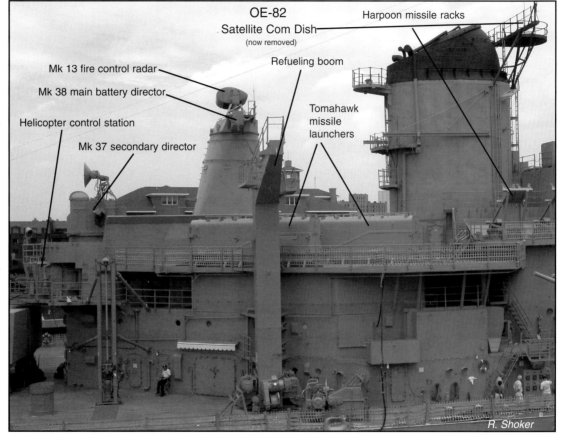

OE-82
Satellite Com Dish
(now removed)

Harpoon missile racks

Mk 13 fire control radar

Refueling boom

Mk 38 main battery director

Tomahawk missile launchers

Helicopter control station

Mk 37 secondary director

R. Shoker

Living and Working Areas

R. Shoker

Armored conning tower

Pilot house

R. Shoker

The Admiral's bridge chair in the flag bridge. The Admiral would often sit here having his morning coffee. The flag officer was a group commander. All Iowas were designed to carry flag officers to command groups of ships. The pilot house is behind the top row of windows surrounding the heavily armored conning tower.

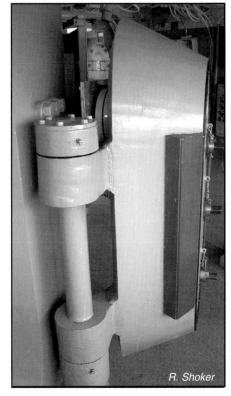

R. Shoker

R. Shoker

The pilot house started out as an open walkway around the conning tower in the Iowa *before being closed in on the other ships. The ship was steered from the inside of the armored conning tower, behind the 17.3 inch thick armored door.*

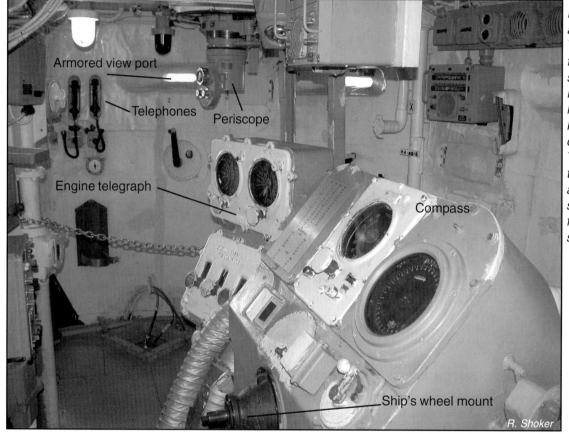

Armored view port

Telephones

Periscope

Engine telegraph

Compass

Ship's wheel mount

R. Shoker

Inside Wisconsin's *armored conning tower. The ship was steered from this location. The ship's wheel has been removed but was located on the spindle located in the lower center of the photo. This area was protected by 17.3 inches of armor, and was designed to withstand the fire from enemy battleships.*

Dom Menta

Dom Menta

Wisconsin *was driven through the sea by four propellers. The inboard (inside) pair had five blades and were 17 feet in diameter. The two outboard propellers had four blades and were 18 feet, 3 inches across.* Wisconsin*'s machinery could generate up to 212,000 shaft horsepower, enough to drive the big ship in excess of 33 knots. The twin rudders were streamlined and semi-balanced and gave excellent performance: the* Iowa*s could outrun smaller escort ships.* Wisconsin *has received her new larger mainmast in this photo from Fall 1953.*

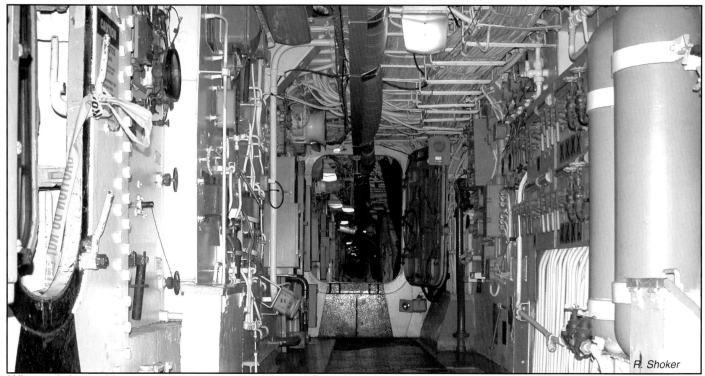

R. Shoker

Wisconsin's *machinery spaces were reached through* Broadway, *the main passageway through the middle of the ship. It was located on the 3rd deck below the armored floor of the 2nd deck. The ship's four engine and four fire (boiler) rooms are located off* Broadway, *as are the generator room, the magazines for the 5-inch guns, and the aft fire control plot. Just visible in the photo is an overhead "I-beam" rail that can be used to move 16-inch shells between turrets 2 and 3 in an emergency.*

Two of Wisky*'s turbo generators.* Wisconsin *received her electric power from eight turbo generators. Paired in twos, they were located in each engine room with their own switch gear. They could produce 1,250 kw of power each. For emergency backup,* Wisconsin *had two diesel-powered 250 kw generators, located fore and aft.*

R. Shoker

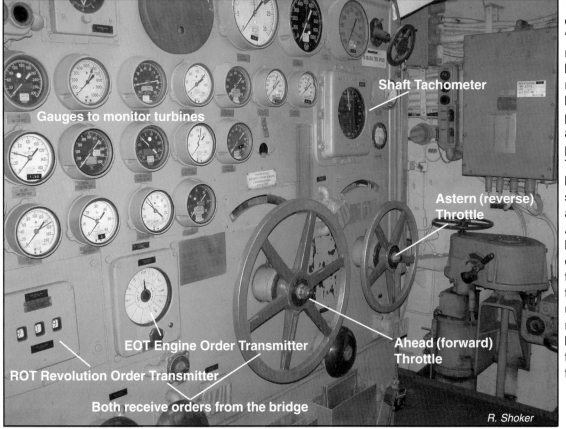

Gauges to monitor turbines

Shaft Tachometer

Astern (reverse) Throttle

Ahead (forward) Throttle

EOT Engine Order Transmitter

ROT Revolution Order Transmitter

Both receive orders from the bridge

R. Shoker

Wisconsin had eight oil-fired boilers in four "fire" rooms. Each fire room contained two boilers and all of their related equipment. The boilers had a working pressure of 634 psi and an operating pressure of 565 psi. The boilers had nine burners each and superheated steam to a temperature of 850°F. As designed, the boilers burned black oil, and the ship's fuel tanks required heaters to heat the fuel before use. In the 1980s rebuild, *Wisconsin*'s boilers were converted to burn modern naval fuel.

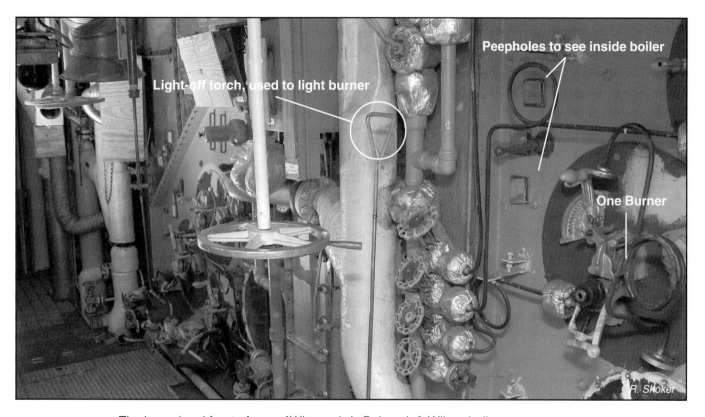

The lower level front of one of Wisconsin*'s Babcock & Wilcox boilers*

Steam turbines

Reduction gear
housing

R. Shoker

The superheated steam from each pair of boilers powered a Westinghouse steam turbine that in turn powered a set of Westinghouse reduction gears. The gears converted the turbine speed to usable horsepower to turn the propeller shafts.

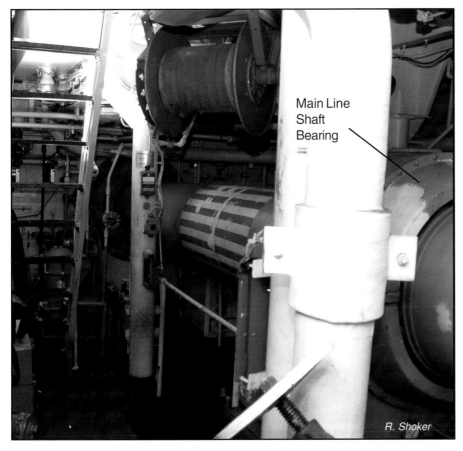

Main Line
Shaft
Bearing

R. Shoker

Deep in the bottom of engine room number 4. To the right is the propeller shaft from engine room number 2, on its way out of the ship. Due to the fact that the engine rooms are staggered, the four propeller shafts are four different lengths. This propeller shaft is about 243 feet long. The brightly colored bands on the shaft make it possible to tell at a glance if the shaft is moving. Visible at the fore end of the shaft is a main line shaft bearing. Bill Henson, who served on Wisconsin in the early fifties, was about to get off watch one day when the # 4 shaft burned up a spring bearing in the aft diesel room. Rather than stop the ship, they slowed the shaft to a stop using the reverse turbine, then locked it into place. He and two other crewmen spent eighty straight backbreaking hours replacing the bearing in a very cramped work area. Because of their efforts, Wisconsin did not have to stop for repairs and continued on her mission.

49

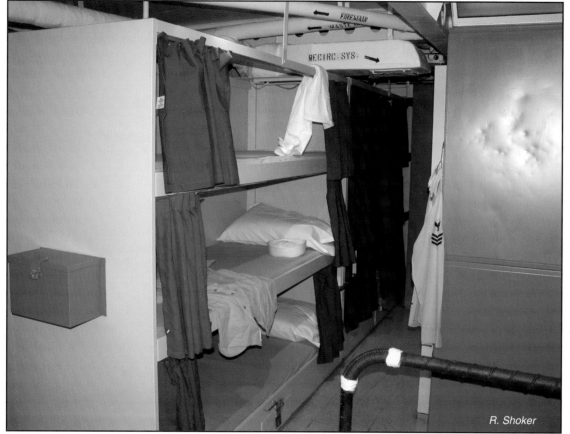

Crew quarters. Wisconsin *originally was equipped with hanging metal bunks for beds, stacked four high. During her 1988 refit her crew was given more modern sleeping arrangements as seen here.* Wisconsin *was designed for a crew of around 1,900 men, but due to the addition of more anti-aircraft guns and electronics, she sailed for war with 2,724 aboard. By the time the war was over, she carried almost 2,900, including her officers, making this once roomy ship very cramped. During her 1988 reactivation, she needed only about 1,600 crewmen.*

R. Shoker

R. Shoker

Crew mess. Wisconsin's crew mess was also upgraded during her 1988 reactivation. Food quality for battleship crews was always good, but sometimes during forward deployments certain supplies like fresh fruits and vegetables would run out. During WWII, Wisconsin's crew ate a daily average of 4,110 pounds of vegetables, 1,640 pounds of fruit, 2,465 pounds of meat, 6,480 eggs, and the all important 1,750 pints of ice cream!

Officers' quarters. They were luxurious compared to the enlisted crew's quarters. Two officers would share the room. They had large lockers (on the right) with two fold-down desks on the right-hand side behind the beds. As designed, Wisconsin *had a complement of about 117 officers. By the end of WWII, that number had risen to 173. During her 1988 reactivation,* Wisconsin *needed only 65 officers.*

R. Shoker

Next Page: *The wardroom where* Wisconsin*'s officers dined, but not the Captain or the Admiral. The angled bulkhead in the left of the photo is the base of the forward funnel.*

R. Shoker

53

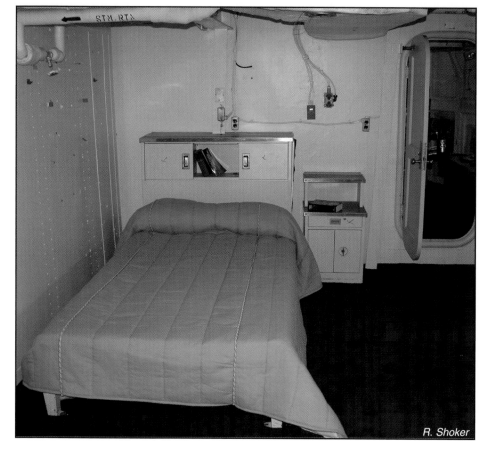

R. Shoker

The Captain's quarters. The Captain, Admiral and Executive Officer each had his own stateroom and a private bathroom (head). The Executive Officer also had a small office, while the Captain had a large private wardroom with a large meeting table. Separating the Captain's and Admiral's area was a private galley, where food was cooked for them and their guests. This is the Captain's sleeping quarters.

The Admiral's dining room (mess). Just visible beyond is the open door leading to the Admiral's cabin, and an open door to his head. The Captain's side is slightly larger, with a conference table used for officers' meetings.

R. Shoker

Forward main battery plotting room. In the foreground is the Mark 41 stable vertical. *It is a gimbaled gyroscope that measures the roll and pitch of the ship and gives that data to the fire control computers. It is also the firing station in the plotting room. Just visible on the front are three pistol-like brass triggers (now covered for preservation) that are used to fire the main guns. The plywood covering is part of the preservation process to protect the glass-covered instruments. Next to that is a* Mark1A *fire control computer. Along the back wall is a portrait of the* Wisconsin *painted by her crew.*

Above: The wiring behind a fire control switch board.

R. Shoker

Right: Fire control switchboard. Hundreds of J-type rotary switches in both the main battery plotting rooms and the secondary plotting rooms allowed for the programming of the ship's fire control system. The switchboards allowed any gun to be directed by any director and any computer to provide fire control data for any gun. This very effective but complex system required a high level of training by the crew to reach combat efficiency.

R. Shoker

R. Shoker

Wisconsin*'s CEC, or Combat Engagement Center. Here is where modern combat is directed. The officer on deck would control the room from the center chair (on the right in this photo). Off to the extreme left are the Tomahawk control stations. During the Gulf War, combat operations were controlled from this room.*

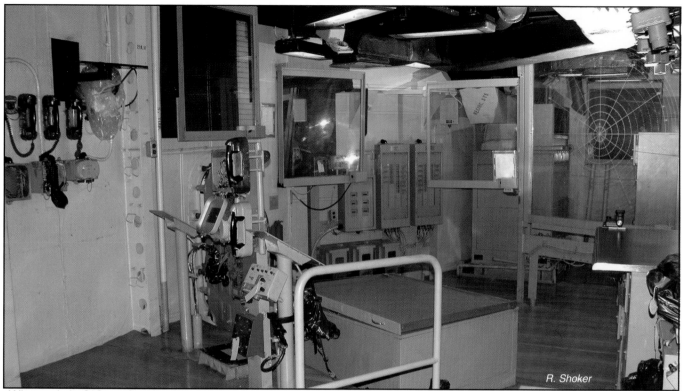

R. Shoker

Wisconsin's *CIC, or Combat Information Center. This room (along with the CEC) was not in the original design of the Iowas but was added during construction (the CEC was added in the 1988 refit). This area was used to direct combat during WWII. Notice the glass plotting grids.*

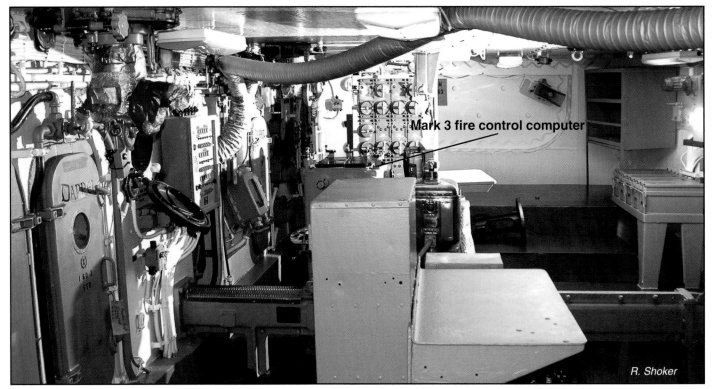

Mark 3 fire control computer

R. Shoker

Inside turret #1. The bulkhead to the left is a firewall between the gun breeches and the rest of the turret. Entry to the gun spaces was though the doors. Each turret had a Mark 3 mechanical fire control computer which allowed the turret to be fired locally if the ship's main fire control systems were knocked out. The turret had a crew of seventy-seven men.

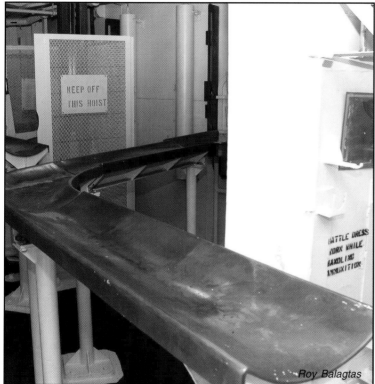

Roy Balagtas

Roy Balagtas

Each gun required six bags of powder to fire. The powder started its journey deep in the ship, being pushed along a brass ramp (to avoid any sparks) to the turret (left). At the base of the turret, the bags were passed though the armor via flash-proof doors (right). It required thirteen men per gun turret to provide enough powder for two rounds per minute per gun.

61

Roy Balagtas

Dom Menta

Once inside the turret, the powder was loaded onto one of three powder hoists (left) where it would be lifted up to the gun breech. Once in the gun breech, it would roll into a tray and be rammed into the chamber behind the giant 16-inch shell. The photo on the right shows a powder bag that has just come out of the hoist in the left of the picture and is getting ready to be rammed into the huge gun. This area is inside the door that is visible on the left in the photo on page 60. (Out of each turret's crew of seventy-seven, thirty were in the gun, four on the electric deck below, thirty men below that in the projectile handling areas and thirteen men to load powder.) Loading and firing the guns was a very complex and precise operation. Wisconsin's turret's operation manual contained almost 500 pages!

Life at Sea

Dom Menta

Crewman Dom Menta took this beautiful portrait of Wisconsin *anchored in the Japanese port of Sasebo, Japan in 1953.*

Richard A. Pestke

Dick Pestke served on the battleships North Carolina *and* Indiana *in WWII before snapping this photo in October 1947.*

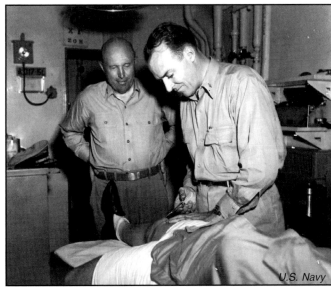

U.S. Navy

Above: Wisconsin *was a city with over 2,000 men on board. She was fully equipped to handle almost any medical emergency, including x-rays and surgery. Here one of* Wisconsin's *men receives stitches to his knee in sickbay.*

Right: *A crewman gets transferred to* Wisconsin *from the guppy submarine* USS Grenadier *via the highline. Much safer than it looks, the highline allowed ships to transfer personnel while underway.*

Dom Menta

Pearson

Imagine having to whip out 4,000 chocolate chip cookies for 2,000 of your closest friends. Wisconsin's bakery was constantly busy meeting the needs of its crew. Wisconsin's ovens would consume an average of 1,500 pounds of flour <u>per day</u> during WWII.

U.S. Navy

R. Shoker

Wisconsin's decks were covered with teak wood -- durable and almost impervious to the harsh environment at sea. The teak provided two valuable services: it acted as an insulation barrier against the hot sun in tropical waters, and secondly, provided a durable and non-skid surface. The wood required constant maintenance. In this photo from the 1950s, the crew is holystoning (rubbing it with sandstone) the deck to clean it. At right is the same section of deck (looking the other way) today.

Dom Menta

Wisconsin*'s CIC in action during this drill from the 1950s. A color photo of this room as it looks today is on page 59.*

Bill Henson

Wisconsin's crew worked hard to make her an efficient fighting machine. There were times, however, to recognize men for extraordinary work. Here is a meritorious Captain's Mast that was held to honor three sailors in engine room number 4 for their difficult 80 straight hour repair of a mainline shaft spring bearing. The sailors are in white and from left to right are Art Olsen, Bill Henson, and Cliff Wilson. See page 49 for the story of the repair.

J.S. NAVY

Dom Menta

Above: *Life on board was not all work. Dom Menta snapped this photo of Dave Haskins resting on a stack of 5-inch powder cans outside the photo lab during his deployment in the 1950s.*

Left: *Crewmen relaxing in their bunks in the 1950s. These are a far cry from the modern bunks on board today (see page 50)*

70

Dom Menta

Dom Menta

There was also time for entertainment. Ed Sullivan and singer June Valli visited the ship in this show for the boys in 1955 while Wisconsin *was in New York (left). The men in the foreground are making sure that* Miss Armed Forces 1953 *does not lose her balance while sitting on one of the 16-inch gun barrels (right).* Wisconsin *was a happy ship, with events like these as reward for hard work helping to keep morale high.*

Here is the sole purpose for the crew's hard work: keeping the big guns on station to defend the nation that created her. Here Wisconsin *blasts targets in North Korea in Spring 1952. This photograph also shows a number of smaller details. The long rail-like device by the number 3 turret is a small portable catapult for* Wisconsin*'s target drones. At the very front of the catapult (at the bottom of the photo) is the small cradle the drone rested on. This photo also shows in detail the large single pole mainmast on the aft funnel. It would be replaced that Fall with a larger, cage-like mast during her refit in the States. The newer mast is visible on page 63.*

Bill Henson

Aircraft

D Yeager

Above: *A Curtiss Seahawk lands in the water and is ready to be picked up by* Wisconsin*'s large aft crane. Note the catch net underneath the front of the aircraft.*

Dom Menta

Above: Wisconsin*'s fantail in the early 1950s crowded with helicopters. The large copters are Sikorsky S-55s and the smaller helicopter just visible to the left is a Bell HTL.*

U.S. Navy battleships and cruisers were designed to carry seaplanes to help spot and correct shellfire. After 1948, the floatplanes were replaced with helicopters. Originally, helicopters were also going to be used for observation. But the rise of the aircraft carrier as an important platform also created the new mission of air rescue. Helicopters excelled at rescuing downed pilots. As technology improved, helicopters evolved into powerful weapons platforms themselves, particularly in the anti-submarine role.

Fixed-Wing Aircraft

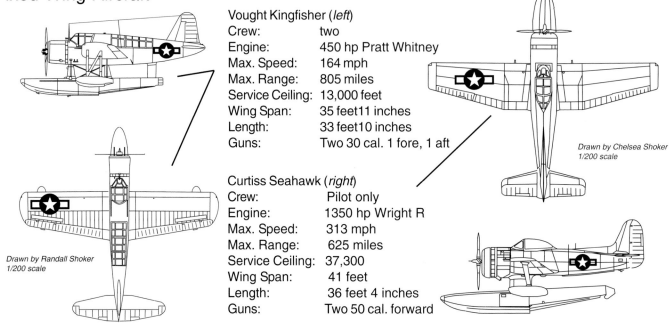

Vought Kingfisher (*left*)

Crew:	two
Engine:	450 hp Pratt Whitney
Max. Speed:	164 mph
Max. Range:	805 miles
Service Ceiling:	13,000 feet
Wing Span:	35 feet 11 inches
Length:	33 feet 10 inches
Guns:	Two 30 cal. 1 fore, 1 aft

Curtiss Seahawk (*right*)

Crew:	Pilot only
Engine:	1350 hp Wright R
Max. Speed:	313 mph
Max. Range:	625 miles
Service Ceiling:	37,300
Wing Span:	41 feet
Length:	36 feet 4 inches
Guns:	Two 50 cal. forward

Drawn by Chelsea Shoker
1/200 scale

Drawn by Randall Shoker
1/200 scale

During WWII, *Wisconsin* carried two different kinds of aircraft: the Vought *Kingfisher* (left), and late in the war, the new Curtiss *Seahawk* (right). The main purpose of *Wisconsin*'s aircraft was to spot her shell fire and to radio corrections back to allow the ship's fire control officers to adjust their fire. They also performed rescue missions as well. The aircraft were carried on two catapults at the stern of the ship and were retrieved from the water by the large crane (now removed) on *Wisconsin*'s fantail.

Naval Helicopters

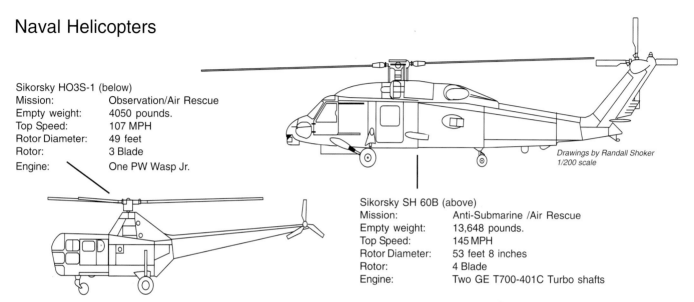

Sikorsky HO3S-1 (below)

Mission:	Observation/Air Rescue
Empty weight:	4050 pounds.
Top Speed:	107 MPH
Rotor Diameter:	49 feet
Rotor:	3 Blade
Engine:	One PW Wasp Jr.

*Drawings by Randall Shoker
1/200 scale*

Sikorsky SH 60B (above)

Mission:	Anti-Submarine /Air Rescue
Empty weight:	13,648 pounds.
Top Speed:	145 MPH
Rotor Diameter:	53 feet 8 inches
Rotor:	4 Blade
Engine:	Two GE T700-401C Turbo shafts

In 1948, the new Sikorsky HO3S-1 began to be used to supplement the Curtiss Seahawk aircraft. By 1948, the floatplanes were gone. *Wisconsin* did not have hangar facilities for helicopters, but there was room for them on her fantail after her catapults were removed. *Wisconsin* carried, or could land every type of Naval helicopter in use during her service. The Sikorsky HO3S-1 was officially listed as an observation aircraft and was particularly useful during the Korean War, operating as the air-rescue arm of *Wisconsin* in helping retrieve downed carrier pilots. During her last deployment, large helicopters like the Sikorsky H-60 Sea Hawk (not to be confused with the Curtiss Seahawk seaplane on page 74) not only fulfilled the air-rescue role, but also its primary mission of anti-submarine warfare. The Sea Hawk could carry two anti-submarine torpedos as well as 25 sonobouys used to help locate the enemy submarines.

Technical Data

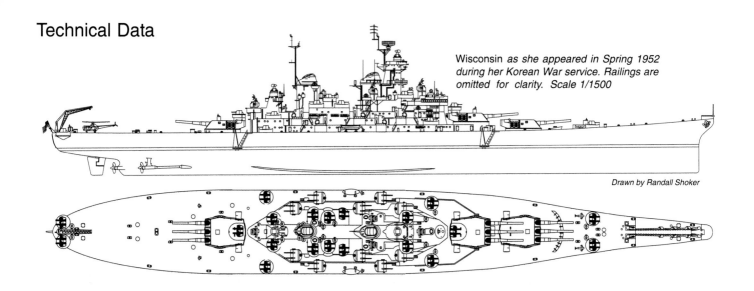

Wisconsin *as she appeared in Spring 1952 during her Korean War service. Railings are omitted for clarity. Scale 1/1500*

Drawn by Randall Shoker

Name and Hull Number:	*Wisconsin* (BB-64)
Builder:	Philadelphia Navy Yard
Laid down:	January 25, 1941
Launched:	December 7, 1943
Commissioned:	April 16, 1944

Dimensions

Length overall:	887 feet 3 inches
Waterline length:	860 feet
Maximum beam:	108 feet 2 inches
Maximum draft:	37 feet 9 inches

Machinery

Wisconsin's *mid-section*

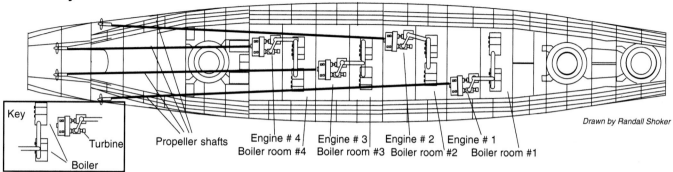

Key

Turbine

Boiler

Propeller shafts

Engine # 4
Boiler room #4

Engine # 3
Boiler room #3

Engine # 2
Boiler room #2

Engine # 1
Boiler room #1

Drawn by Randall Shoker

Boilers:	Eight Babcock & Wilcox three drum express type equipped with two furnaces and double uptakes Pressure 565 PSI at 850 degrees F.
Turbines:	Four sets of Westinghouse geared turbines
Shaft horsepower:	212,000 forward 44,000 astern
Maximum speed:	in excess of 33 knots
Generators:	Eight ship's service turbo generators (1,250 kw) Two emergency diesel generators (250 kw) Total ship's service capacity: 10,000 kw, 450 Volts, AC

Center section armor

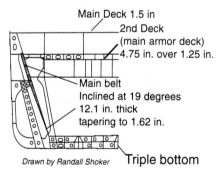

Main Deck 1.5 in
2nd Deck
(main armor deck)
4.75 in. over 1.25 in.

Main belt
Inclined at 19 degrees
12.1 in. thick
tapering to 1.62 in.

Triple bottom

Drawn by Randall Shoker

Dom Menta

Navy Photographer Dom Menta (foreground) and Marvin Fulton work on an enlarger in the photo lab in the 1950s. If you look closely you can see an image of Wisconsin *on the plate. Mr. Menta is the webmaster for* Wisconsin*'s crew association webpage. You can see his excellent work at* www.usswisconsin.org.

Acknowledgements

I would like to thank the Hampton Roads Naval Historical Foundation (HRNHF), its director Jake Tobin RADM USN (ret), Mary Mosier, Operations Manager of *USS Wisconsin* and Curator Joe Judge who, along with Gordon Calhoun, Tom Dandes, and Robert Fall, all put in long hours of checking facts and figures. Thanks also to Roy Balagtas and my son Alex for helping me photograph the ship. Thanks to my daughter Chelsea for her drawings, and Sally Tobin, Becky Poulliot, my wife Nancy, and my text editor William Fisher for their proofing work.

Thanks to former crewmen Perry Bodnar, Barry Cordwell, Bill Henson, George Kent, Richard Pestke, Hector Santiago, Frank Saraicone, and. D. Yeager for allowing me to use their photos.

A special thanks to former *Wisconsin* crew member Dom Menta. Dom's generous help with research was matched only by the photos he contributed to this book. Thanks Dom.

Thanks to all of you,
Randall Shoker

This dramatic shot of water misting over the bow was captured by Dom Menta during his service in the 1950s.

References

The Daybook* edited by Gordon Calhoun
The Iowa Class Battleships* by Malcom Muir
United States Navy Aircraft since 1911
by Gordon Swanborough, Peter M. Bowers
The Two Ocean War* by Samuel Eliot Morison
Naval Weapons of World War II by John Campbell
Iowa Class Battleships, Their Design, Weapons & Equipment*
by Robert F. Sumrall/ Thomas Walkowiak
Forward for Freedom: The Story of Battleship Wisconsin:
by Amy Waters Yarsinske
U.S. Battleships in Action, Part II by Robert C. Stern
The U.S.S. Wisconsin: A History of Two Battleships by Richard H. Zeitlin
United States' Battleships in World War II *
by Robert O. Dulin, Jr., William H. Garzke, Jr.
U.S. Battleships: An Illustrated Design History* by Norman Friedman
* highly recommended for further reading.

World Wide Web references
US. Coastguard: www.uscg.mil
U.S. Navy History: www.history.navy.mil
Vyacheslav Ryzhenkov's website at www.thetankmaster.com

Special thanks to:
David R. Scheu, Sr.
Captian USN (Ret.)
Former Operations Officer of Battleship *New Jersey*

Visit USS Wisconsin!

The Hampton Roads Naval Museum and the entrance to Battleship *Wisconsin* are located on the second floor of Nauticus: The National Maritime Center in downtown Norfolk, Virginia. Admission is free to the museum and ship. There is no on-site parking, but the City operates parking garages within walking distance. Call 757-322-2987 to arrange group visits.

Visit the Hampton Roads Naval Museum online at http://www.hrnm.navy.mil

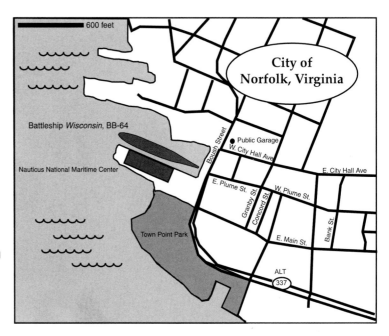

600 feet

City of Norfolk, Virginia

Battleship *Wisconsin*, BB-64

Public Garage

Boush Street

W. City Hall Ave

E. City Hall Ave

Nauticus National Maritime Center

E. Plume St.

Granby St.

Concord St.

W. Plume St.

Bank St.

Town Point Park

E. Main St.

ALT 337

Hours
Summer (Memorial Day to Labor Day): Open Daily: 10 am to 6 pm.
Non-Summer: Tuesday-Saturday: 10 am to 5 pm, Sunday: 12 pm to 5pm, closed Monday.
Closed Thanksgiving Day, Christmas Eve, Christmas Day.